Sports
Technology

by Geoff Thompson

NELSON
CENGAGE Learning™

Australia • Brazil • Japan • Korea • Mexico • Singapore • Spain • United Kingdom • United States

Contents

Introduction

Nearly everything we do in our lives involves *technology* — including sport. Technology helps today's sports people go faster, higher and further than before.

How fast would today's athletes run on dirt tracks in bare feet? What kind of injuries would happen without helmets and protective gear? How often would we watch a game of football or cricket if it wasn't on television?

Technology improves sports clothing, footwear, sports fields, racquets, bats, balls, helmets, padding and timing equipment. It also makes it easier and more fun to watch sports. With modern stadiums and television technology, spectators can get a much better view of the action.

Chapter 1

Tools of the trade

Sports people are always trying to improve their performance. They look for every advantage they can find. Better fitness, healthier food and more practice might give them an edge over their opponents. Sometimes they can get that edge with better equipment.

In the past, most sports equipment was made from wood, leather and other natural *materials*. Even bicycle wheels were once made of wood! But over the years, new materials and new designs have improved sports equipment.

Now we have materials such as *fibreglass*, plastic, *aluminium*, and *carbon fibre*. These materials are lighter, stronger and more *flexible*.

Nearly all sports equipment uses modern materials. Can you think of any sports equipment that has always been made of the same material?

Dick Fosbury was the famous high jumper who invented the 'Fosbury flop'.

Today high jumpers wear streamlined clothing, the poles are more flexible, and the landing mat prevents injury. A camera attached to the high jump records the action.

Playing equipment

The design of sports equipment is always improving. Early tennis racquets had a small head with a thick wooden frame. Now they have big heads and strong, narrow frames made of aluminium or carbon fibre.

An old racquet.

A modern racquet.

The strings used to be made of cat gut, but now they are *nylon*. Tennis players have more power and control over their shots when they use modern racquets. The top players serve a lot harder and faster than they used to!

Hockey sticks used to be made of wood. Now the wood is covered in fibreglass to add strength and flexibility. Some hockey sticks are made from carbon fibre, and some have aluminium handles.

? DID YOU KNOW?

Years ago, pole vaulting was a risky sport. The wooden poles often snapped because of the pole vaulter's weight. Now the poles are made of fibreglass. The new poles are much lighter, stronger and more flexible.

Chapter 2

Clothing and protective gear

A lot of sports clothing is made from synthetic materials. The right type of clothing can make athletes more comfortable and maybe even a little faster — and every little bit counts!

Many different kinds of athletes wear *Lycra*®. Lycra® is lightweight, stretchy and tight-fitting so it doesn't flap around. Smooth clothes like this don't slow you down.

Surfers and scuba divers need clothing that will keep them warm in the water. They wear wetsuits made from a type of foam called 'neoprene'.

? DID YOU KNOW?

'Gore-tex®' is a very advanced material used in waterproof jackets. It stops the rain getting in, but it also allows the body's perspiration to get out. It keeps the wearer warm and dry. It is used by climbers, skiers, mountaineers, and many other types of sports people.

Shoes

At the very first Olympics more than 2000 years ago, the athletes wore no shoes at all. As time went by, runners began to wear shoes made of leather. Since then, sports shoes have come a long way. *Synthetic* materials such as plastic, hard-wearing foam and rubber are now used for sports shoes.

Most sports have their own special shoes. Each type of shoe is designed to give the right amount of grip and comfort. Indoor sports require shoes with smooth, flat soles for polished floors. Football boots have tough plastic soles with studs to grip on grassy fields.

The soles of modern running shoes are made of hard-wearing foam and rubber. The soft sole acts like a shock-absorber. It squashes under pressure and then returns to its original shape. This helps to look after your feet, legs and back.

Football boots have studs to help prevent players from falling over.

Ski boots have thick plastic on the outside. This makes them strong and keeps the wet snow out.

Track shoes have spikes to grip the surface of the running track.

Protective gear

Bumps, falls, hits and crashes often happen in some sports. Good protective gear makes many sports safer to play.

Padding is made for different parts of the body – helmets for the head, mouth guards for teeth, guards for the wrists, elbows, knees and shins, and gloves for the hands.

Sports padding has a soft, light, spongy material such as foam on the inside. The tough outer layer is often made from plastic.

Helmets are especially important because they protect the head. Different sports have different types of helmets. The helmets for cycling, skateboarding, field hockey, ice hockey, cricket, American football, fencing, softball and baseball are designed specially for that particular sport.

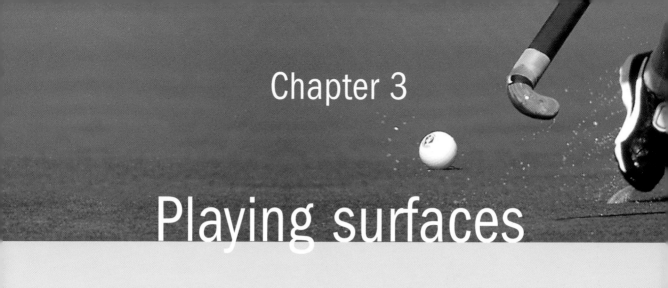

Chapter 3

Playing surfaces

Grass is an ideal playing surface. It's soft and can be mown or rolled to make a smooth, even surface. But grass does have some disadvantages. It can get soggy, lumpy or muddy. These things make it more difficult to play the game.

Artificial grass has helped to fix some of these problems. It is used on tennis courts, hockey fields, American football and soccer fields. The surface is smooth, even and easy to run on. It lasts for a long time and it doesn't matter what the weather is like. Sport can be played on artificial grass all year round.

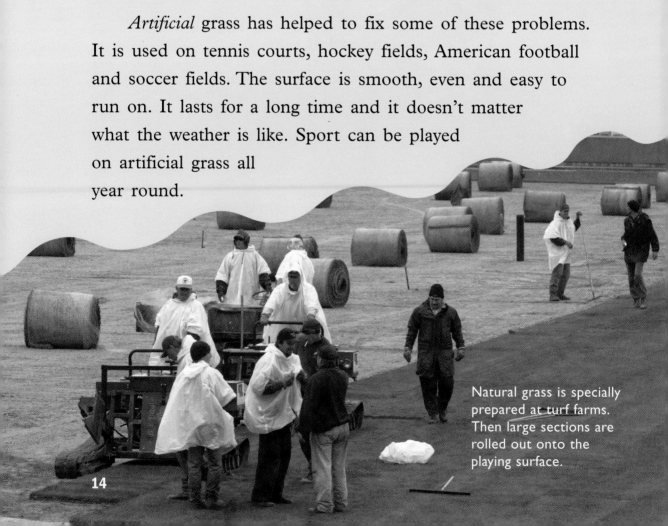

Natural grass is specially prepared at turf farms. Then large sections are rolled out onto the playing surface.

?

DID YOU KNOW?

Artificial grass is made from long thick plastic fibres woven together like a carpet.

How to prevent injury

In very active sports athletes do a lot of running, jumping, side-stepping, pivoting and sudden stopping. If they do this on a hard surface, there is a greater risk that they will hurt their ankles and knees. Many sports fields are now made with materials that are softer on the athletes' feet and legs.

Netball and basketball courts and gymnasiums have wooden floors that are 'sprung'. This means that they have a spongy material under the floor boards. Artificial grass and synthetic tennis courts also have layers of *elastic* material under them.

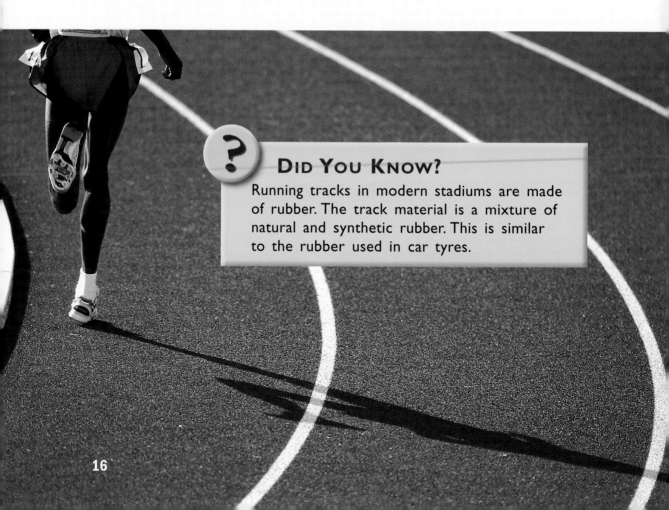

? DID YOU KNOW?
Running tracks in modern stadiums are made of rubber. The track material is a mixture of natural and synthetic rubber. This is similar to the rubber used in car tyres.

Chapter 4

Large equipment

Many years ago, bicycles were not designed for comfort or speed. They used to have hard leather seats with no padding, solid rubber tyres, and they had no chains or gears. The frames were made of heavy metal or wood. They were difficult to push around. Imagine if you had to ride one of these to school!

A modern mountain bike

foam padding on seat

metal alloy frame

suspension system

lots of gears to make it easier to ride up and down hills

rubber inner tubes

thick rubber tyres to go over bumps and rough ground easily

But today, technology has solved these problems. Seats have springs and foam padding. The tyres are made of hard-wearing rubber. They have rubber inner tubes that are filled with air. Modern bikes have strong, light, metal *alloy* frames. Some mountain bikes have suspension systems on both front and rear wheels.

Olympic racing bikes are built for speed and are very hi-tech. Their frames are made from carbon fibre. These bikes are specially shaped to move through the air more easily. They have a smooth, *streamlined* surface. The front forks are shaped like the wing of an aeroplane. The wheels are solid instead of having metal spokes.

? DID YOU KNOW?

The best equipment doesn't always mean victory. Strong, tight clips are designed to hold cyclists' feet firmly in place on the pedals. However, when champion cyclist Shane Kelly competed for a gold medal in the Atlanta Olympics in 1996, somehow his foot slipped from the pedal, costing him the race.

Fibreglass and carbon fibre

Fibreglass and carbon fibre have some big advantages over traditional materials. They are light, very flexible and they can be easily made into just about any shape. This makes them ideal for large sports equipment such as rowing boats, speed boats, surfboards and sports wheelchairs.

? DID YOU KNOW?

Originally surfboards were made from slabs of wood. They were often heavier than the surfers using them. Modern surfboards can weigh as little as ten kilograms.

Fibreglass and carbon fibre are made by combining two different materials. One material is a cloth made from strong threads of glass or carbon. The other material is a *resin* — a liquid that sets into a hard, tough plastic. The cloth is soaked and covered with resin to make carbon fibre or fibreglass. The result is a much stronger material than either the cloth or the resin by themselves.

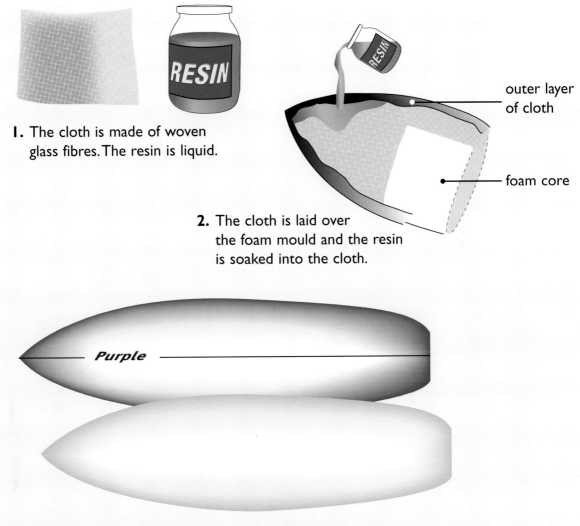

1. The cloth is made of woven glass fibres. The resin is liquid.

outer layer of cloth

foam core

2. The cloth is laid over the foam mould and the resin is soaked into the cloth.

Purple

3. The resin sets, and makes hard, strong fibreglass.

Chapter 5

Electronic timing systems

In many races the difference between first and second place can be just a fraction of a second.

It's very hard for the human eye to tell the difference between first and second place in a close finish. So modern technology has found the answer to this problem — electronic timing devices.

In athletics, a computer system links a pad on the starting blocks with the starter's gun. If a runner leaves the blocks too early, the computer detects a 'false' start and the competitors are recalled to start the race again.

Swimming pools have sensitive pads at each end that register the instant they are touched by the swimmer. The touch pads are linked to a computer which records the time. A touch pad on the diving block also detects 'false' starts. This system is far more accurate than hand-held stopwatches.

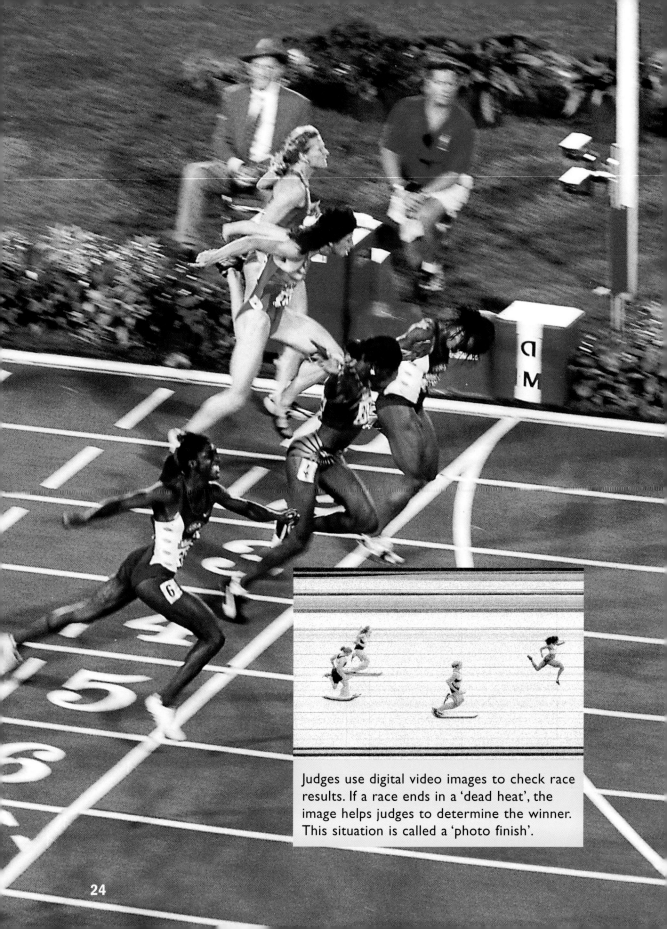

Judges use digital video images to check race results. If a race ends in a 'dead heat', the image helps judges to determine the winner. This situation is called a 'photo finish'.

Downhill skiers and bobsled riders race down a course one at a time. The timing of each competitor must be very accurate. This is done by pointing a laser beam across the finish line. The laser is connected to a clock that records the times of every competitor to the nearest millisecond.

Track races are timed with a digital video system. A video camera records the runners as they cross the finish line. It takes a photograph at every one hundredth of a second. Each photo frame has the split-second time written on it. The judge stops the video replay and reads the time as each runner crosses the line.

Marathon runners have a silicon chip tied to their shoelaces. The chip contains the runner's name in a numbered code. When the runner crosses the start and finish lines, an antenna 'reads' the code on the chip. A computer calculates how long it took each runner to finish the race.

Chapter 6

Watching sport

Some people like to go to a game and see the action as it happens. Some people prefer to sit on the couch at home and watch it on television. Either way, modern technology makes it easier for people to see and enjoy their favourite sport.

? DID YOU KNOW?

Some stadiums have roofs that slide open and close, depending on the weather. They can let the sunshine in or keep the rain out.

Dear Grandpa,

I went with my friend Sam to see a one-day cricket game last week. The atmosphere in the stadium was very exciting. There were thousands of spectators. Our seats were high up in the grandstand and we had a great view of the game. There were six giant light stands. The lights came on when it got dark — it was almost as bright as daylight! There were giant TV screens at each end of the field. They showed replays of all the action. It was great fun and my team won!

Love, Jo

Watching in comfort

Many years ago, the only way to see sport was to go to
the sports field. There were no televisions and no live action
replays. If you didn't see it live, then you didn't see it at all.
But with today's technology, you can see more sport than
you could possibly wish for. You can watch your favourite
sport on television, or you can record it on video and
play it back later. Some sports are even broadcast
over the Internet.

With communications technology, television images can be sent via a *satellite* from one side of the world to the other. Live action can be filmed in one place and appear a split second later on television screens around the world.

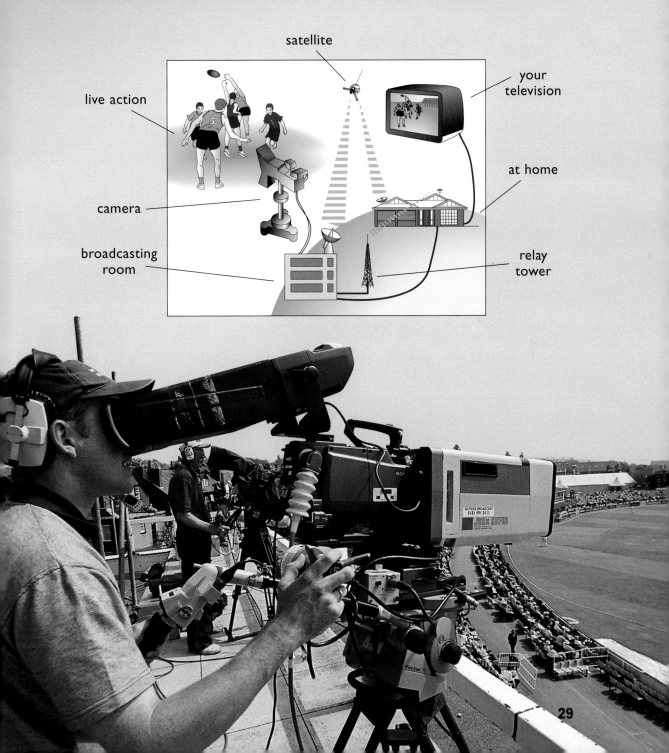

satellite

your television

live action

at home

camera

broadcasting room

relay tower

Chapter 7

Technology of the future

In the last hundred years technology has made many changes to sport. What changes will it make in the next hundred years?

Maybe human referees will be replaced by robots that never make a mistake. Perhaps new materials will be developed so that sports clothes automatically cool the athletes when they get hot, or warm them when they cool down. One day we might have televisions that allow us to choose the camera angle or the action replay that we want to see.

Whatever the new developments are, technology is sure to play an important role in the future of sport.

How do you think sport will be improved by technology in the future?

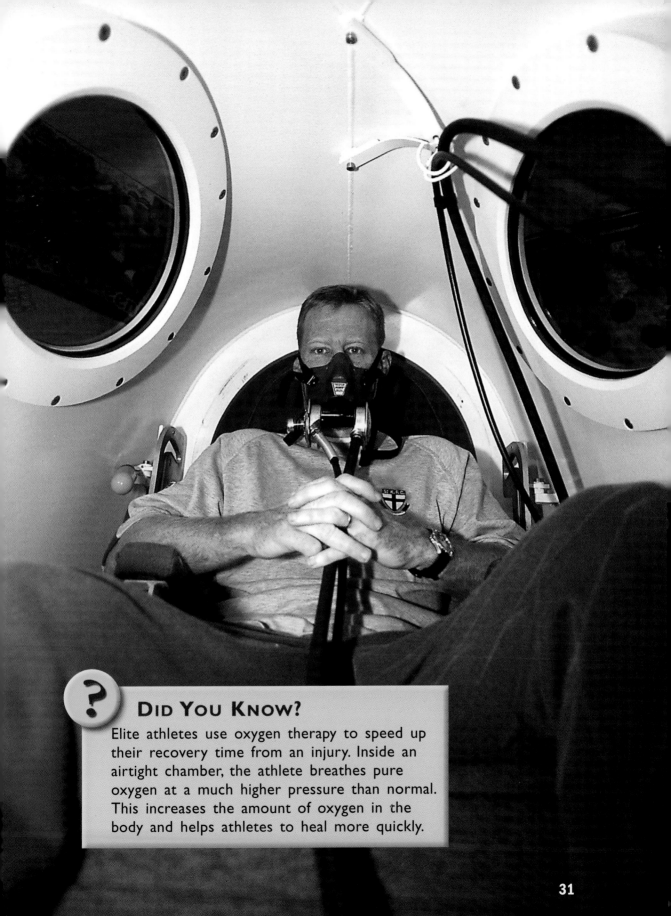

? DID YOU KNOW?

Elite athletes use oxygen therapy to speed up their recovery time from an injury. Inside an airtight chamber, the athlete breathes pure oxygen at a much higher pressure than normal. This increases the amount of oxygen in the body and helps athletes to heal more quickly.

Glossary

alloy	strong, light metal that is made by melting and mixing other metals together
aluminium	a strong, light metal
artificial	not natural
carbon fibre	a strong, light material made by combining carbon cloth and a plastic resin
elastic	soft and stretchy
fibreglass	a strong, light material made by weaving strands of glass together and cementing them with a resin
flexible	able to bend easily
Lycra®	a stretchy fabric made from nylon
materials	materials such as plastics, wood, metal, fibreglass and rubber that we use to make or build things
nylon	a synthetic material
resin	a special type of plastic
satellite	a machine that orbits the Earth and receives and sends television signals
streamlined	smoothly shaped to move through the air or water easily
synthetic	a material such as nylon that has not been made from natural fibres
technology	tools and processes we use to solve problems

Further reading

Hammond, Jim. *Sport*. Collins Eyewitness, 1998.

Smith, Nigel. *Then and Now Sport*. Franklin Watts Books, 1996.

Thompson, Geoff. *Sports Technology*. Nelson Infotexts, Nelson ITP, 1998.